Published in the UK by Scholastic, 2024
1 London Bridge, London, SE1 9BG
Scholastic Ireland, 89E Lagan Road,
Dublin Industrial Estate, Glasnevin,
Dublin, D11 HP5F

Text © Scholastic, 2024
Illustrations by Jason Cox © Scholastic, 2024

ISBN 978 0702 33884 7

A CIP catalogue record for this book is available
from the British Library.

Printed and bound in the
UK by Bell and Bain Ltd, Glasgow

Paper made from wood grown in sustainable
forests and other controlled sources.

1 3 5 7 9 10 8 6 4 2

www.scholastic.co.uk

A Little Bit of
Positivity

Potatoes, Peppers
and Pineapples to Make Your Day

SCHOLASTIC

Be gentle
to yourself
today.

I think you're pear-fect the way you are.

You're
cute and
capable of
anything.

Everything about you is good vibes.

What's round, cute and believes in you? This little potato!

Tough times
make you
stronger.

Every day
is a new
start.

You deserve to be
peppered with love
and support.

I'm a teeny tomato and
I think you're fabulous.

I'm a little pickle and I'll always pick you.

I'm a small pineapple and I
think you look great today.

Happiness never
decreases by
being shared.

Buddha

This
pickle
says
'hello!'

This little butternut squash thinks you're strong and full of courage.

Life can be
fruitful after
persevering.

I hope you have
the best day ever!

If you're
feeling sad,
remember
that tomorrow
is always a
fresh start.

Life is
a journey,
not a
destination.

Changes can
happen at
any moment
and it's okay.

It's utterly
fine to
fall down
sometimes.

This little potato is
cheering for you.

I think
you're as
cool as a
cucumber.

Just remember
that you
are loved.

It does not matter
how slowly you go
as long as you
do not stop.

Confucius

You are right
where you
need to be.

Everyone needs to be ready for your awesomeness!

Remember
to celebrate all
your achievements.

I think you're
fantastic and
deserve the
world.

The heart that loves
is always young.

Greek Proverb

Being perfect is not a goal, being you is enough.

Put your best foot forward.

You're a star and your
future is bright.

I'm sending you positivity from my head tomatoes.

Do the things
that make you
happy.

I believe
you'll reach
every goal
you make.

I have a feeling that it will all be alright.

If you get scared, remember that all it takes is one sprout of courage.

It's okay to take some time to rest and recover.

You are
on the
right path.

You don't have to face all your problems alone.

You can overcome any obstacle in your way.

Never be sorry
for being your
awesome self.

True friends will be there for when
you feel upside down.

There is always someone here to root for you.

Find one
thing that
gives you
joy today.

Your feelings are valid — don't let anyone tell you otherwise.

On days you feel
like a small fry, just
know that you're
ready for anything.

I know you have the strength to power through!